Science Fiction Collections

Vistas – Chris Kelso

Horror Fiction Collections

Distant Frequencies – Frank Duffy
Where We Live – Tim Cooke
Night Voices – Paul Edwards & Frank Duffy

Anthologies

The Darkest Battlefield – Tales Of WW1/Horror

DEMAIN PUBLISHING

<u>Short Sharp Shocks!</u>

Book 0: Dirty Paws - Dean M. Drinkel

Book 1: Patient K - Barbie Wilde

Book 2: The Stranger & The Ribbon – Tim Dry

Book 3: Asylum Of Shadows – Stephanie Ellis

Book 4: Monster Beach – Ritchie Valentine Smith

Book 5: Beasties & Other Stories – Martin Richmond

Book 6: Every Moon Atrocious – Emile-Louis Tomas Jouvet

Book 7: A Monster Met – Liz Tuckwell

Book 8: The Intruders & Other Stories – Jason D. Brawn

Book 9: The Other – David Youngquist

Book 10: Symphony Of Blood – Leah Crowley

Book 11: Shattered – Anthony Watson

Book 12: The Devil's Portion – Benedict J. Jones

Book 13: Cinders Of A Blind Man Who Could See – Kev Harrison

Book 14: Dulce Et Decorum Est – Dan Howarth

Book 15: Blood, Bears & Dolls – Allison Weir

Book 16: The Forest Is Hungry – Chris Stanley

Book 17: The Town That Feared Dusk – Calvin Demmer

Book 18: Night Of The Rider – Alyson Faye

Book 19: Isidora's Pawn – Erik Hofstatter

Book 20: Plain – D.T. Griffith

Book 21: Supermassive Black Mass – Matthew Davis

Book 22: Whispers Of The Sea (& Other Stories) – L. R. Bonehill

Book 23: Magic – Eric Nash
Book 24: The Plague – R.J. Meldrum
Book 25: Candy Corn – Kevin M. Folliard
Book 26: The Elixir – Lee Allen Howard
Book 27: Breaking The Habit – Yolanda Sfetsos
Book 28: Forfeit Tissue – C. C. Adams
Book 29: Crown Of Thorns – Trevor Kennedy
Book 30: The Encampment / Blood Memory –
         Zachary Ashford
Book 31: Dreams Of Lake Drukka / Exhumation –
         Mike Thorn
Book 32: Apples / Snail Trails – Russell Smeaton
Book 33: An Invitation To Darkness – Hailey Piper
Book 34: The Necessary Evils & Sick Girl – Dan
         Weatherer
Book 35: The Couvade – Joe Koch
Book 36: The Camp Creeper & Other Stories – Dave
         Jeffery
Book 37: Flaying Sins – Ian Woodhead
Book 38: Hearts & Bones – Theresa Derwin
Book 39: The Unbeliever & The Intruder – Morgan
         K. Tanner
Book 40: The Coffin Walk – Richard Farren Barber
Book 41: The Straitjacket In The Woods – Kitty R.
         Kane
Book 42: Heart Of Stone – M. Brandon Robbins
Book 43: Bits – R.A. Busby
Book 44: Last Meal In Osaka & Other Stories – Gary
         Buller
Book 45: The One That Knows No Fear – Steve
         Stred
Book 46: The Birthday Girl & Other Stories –
         Christopher Beck

Book 47: Crowded House & Other Stories - S.J. Budd
Book 48: Hand To Mouth – Deborah Sheldon
Book 49: Moonlight Gunshot Mallet Flame / A Little Death – Alicia Hilton
Book 50: Dark Corners - David Charlesworth

<u>Murder! Mystery! Mayhem!</u>

Maggie Of My Heart – Alyson Faye
The Funeral Birds – Paula R.C. Readman
Cursed – Paul M. Feeney
The Bone Factory – Yolanda Sfetsos
Garland Cove – Deborah Sheldon
Death In The Dugout – Bruce Harris

<u>Beats! Ballads! Blank Verse!</u>

Book 1: Echoes From An Expired Earth – Allen Ashley
Book 2: Grave Goods – Cardinal Cox
Book 3: From Long Ago – Paul Woodward
Book 4: Laws Of Discord – William Clunie
Book 5: Fanged Dandelion – Eric LaRocca
Book 6: Halloween's Best Cellar – Martin Richmond
Book 7: Existential Jibber Jabber – Marc Shapiro

<u>Weird! Wonderful! Other Worlds</u>

Book 1: The Raven King – Liz Tuckwell
Book 2: The Wired City – Yolanda Sfetsos

<u>Horror Novels & Novellas</u>

House Of Wrax – Raven Dane

And Blood Did Fall – Chad A. Clark
The Fallen – Anthony Watson
The Underclass – Dan Weatherer
Cheslyn Myre – Dan Weatherer
Greenbeard – John Travis
Tower Of Raven – Kevin M. Folliard
Welcome Home Natalie – Reyna Young
Little Bird – TR Hitchman
Society Place – Andrew David Barker
Axe – Terry Grimwood
Wicked Blood – E.C. Hanson
Between The Teeth Of Charon – Grant Longstaff
The Again-Walkers – Deborah Sheldon

Science Fiction Novels & Novellas

Odyssey Of The Black Turtle – Paul Woodward
Sons Of Sol – Kevin R. McNally

The 'A QUIET APOCALYPSE' Series

A Quiet Apocalypse – Dave Jeffery
Cathedral (A Quiet Apocalypse Book 2) – Dave Jeffery
The Samaritan (A Quiet Apocalypse Book 3) – Dave Jeffery
A Silent Dystopia (Stories Of A Quiet Apocalypse) – Edited by D.T. Griffith
Tribunal (A Quiet Apocalypse Book 4) – Dave Jeffery

General Fiction

Joe – Terry Grimwood
Finding Jericho – Dave Jeffery

EXISTENTIAL JIBBER JABBER

POEMS BY
MARC SHAPIRO

A BEATS! BALLADS! BLANK VERSE! BOOK

BOOK 7

CONTENTS

CHALK TALK

Chalk bites into the street
Flaking crumbs as it travels
To the elbow
To the muddied Air Jordans
Past blue jeaned bent and twisted leg
Past a raw, bloodied pulpy spot
Around a body twisted in half
Finally coming to outline at the head
Eyes closed
Mouth open in silent scream
As blood and brain matter dot a horrid i
The sheet comes up
Over legs
Blotting out a future
Over body
Cutting short conscience
Over the head and gone
As the world dies screaming
Leaving only chalk

TECHNICAL KNOCKOUT IN TESTOSTERONE HELL

She walked into the Mexican bar
Chest straining against thin, silky cloth
Hips doing the jump dance
Face blonde on blonde
Slightly used around the edges
Bathed in red-black light
And bullfighting posters
She was not easy
But any man with a smile
A line
And the price of a drink
Could have had her on any night
Except this one
Because this night was fight night
And the men were directing their lust
toward TV screens
Glowering down with two middleweights
Throwing punches
Drawing blood
Cracking nose cartilage
She sighed
Knowing this night she could not give it
away

So she downed the last drink she had
bought herself
Shook her ass one more time at the
disinterested crowd
And wandered out into the night
Alone
Untouched
As the men cheered a fifth round TKO

I'VE SEEN THE MEN ON MONDAY MORNING

I've seen the men on Monday morning
Crouched over Formica tables
Fighting off the cold
With coffee
Black
They are without women
But they are not alone
Because they have their memories
Of the nights they danced the Lindy
To the beat of a big swing band
When the Dodgers were still in Brooklyn
When they came marching home
triumphant
From the war to end all wars
They have come through life sporting
medals
Elegant scars
Now they drink their coffee
Black
In true grace
As they wait out the end of time

SHE

She used to like to do it in the morning
When sunlight knifed through curtains
Highlighting her movements
Cat like
Like cool, easy jazz
One day something left her
Died
A single tear tarnishing cheek
Rolled down
Moving her into the dark
Where she continues to do it
In silhouette
In emptiness
Alone

DANCES WITH DANGEROUS WOMEN

When I was young
The army spat me out
Shot from guns
Full of disrespect
High on testosterone
And stupidity
So I did the dance with dangerous women
One had sad eyes
Who was on a downward spiral
She was flattered
But warned me off
With tales of a husband
Who battered her soul
And carried big guns
A hair trigger
Yet another came on vulnerable
Hard and heavy
With child and husband
We ran off to Vegas
Fell in love
Her husband smacked her around
She waved the white flag
Nursing her bruises
And went back to him

3 a.m. bred desperation
With a hell spawn waif woman
Whose idea of foreplay
Was to balance a knife on my Adam's Apple
And press down
To just this side of blood
And eternity
The tango lasted just long enough
For her to get bored
And for me to realize
That one day the knife might slip
The worst possible line snagged another
Who rocked my world
Before calmly announcing that her old man
A drug dealer of note
Had just scored big time
And was coming back to town
I shuddered
Thanked her for the good times
And booked
Shell shocked
Up to here with the idea
That the wild life was getting a bit too wild
A little too edgy
Then it got really strange
As the most dangerous name on my dance
card decided to pay a call
She offered love

She offered commitment
But there was a catch
She wanted the same in return
I took a deep breath
And a hesitant first step into the unknown

GIRL LEARNS

Young girl in the crowd
Wants something
Not the usual thing
She wasn't literary gash
Who would tumble for any guy with a
chapbook
Or bored high society
Looking for cheap thrills on the wild side
There was something else
Behind those strong, slanted eyes
Determination
Defiance
And a whole lot of angry
She would go down
But she would not go down easy
A deal was struck over cheap wine
And a tongue kiss
The young girl would give it up
And so would i
My thing became her thing
Sex was carnal
Selfish
Unrewarding
Her optimism turned
From pastels

To cynical blacks
Spirit turned hard
Crass
The color of a bad night swigging Jack
When she would erupt, explode
And strike out
I would wipe the blood off my lips
Shove a pencil and paper in her face
And scream at her to get the bile down
Where it counted
Finally
When I could not turn her any further
I kicked her out
With a look that said 'you're ready'
She turned to me
Looking much like me
And told me to fuck off and die
I smiled
Operation a success
Patient lives
Young girl on the stage
Flipping off the world with electric vision
Apocalyptic images
And words forged in the fires of hell
Spots a young boy in the crowd
Who wants something

WHORE

There's a little bit of whore in all of us
Yeah, I know
We like to think of it as nobler stuff
So we dress it up in compromise
But in our heart of hearts
We all know
That we spread for something
Bend over for someone
And take it until we bleed
But we do it willingly
Because if we didn't
We'd be on the outside looking in
And you can't be a whore
If nobody knows your name

CHOW

How hungry is hungry?
That is the question
Would you swallow it whole?
Gnash it into bite sized bits?
Allow that it tastes like chicken?
Pray as it melts in your mouth?
Gag as it turns suddenly foul?
Like bad essence of roadkill?
If they killed it
Cut it up
Would you eat it?
Life
Food
It's all the same

DRUMS

Hear the drums
Rearing up like a beast
Out of the veldt
The reservation
The commune
The beat house
Spitting percussive fire
Melting inhibitions
With echoing tom toms, snaps and pops
Sending corporate predators out of the slag
heap
Out of the cities
Back to the primitive
Those dancing, swirling, prehistoric places
And into the night
Where the only real voice
Is the drums

STREET LIFE FLICKERS

There were screams in the night
They were close
One thing was certain
They were pissed
Hopped up on pandemic isolation
Protest anger
And yet another day of this is as good as it
gets
F bombs fell like raindrops
Punctuated by
"So, I'm a black Mexican, so what!"
"I think it's time for a race war!"
And for good measure
"Fuck you, you motherfucker!"
Then a neighbor
All right wing, redneck and NRA
Lumbered across the street
And into the fray
They were disturbing his equally listless life
And he had heard enough
He told them to shut the fuck up
And they did
On his way back to his dump he muttered
"I ain't going to stand for any of that racist
shit on our street!"

It was tough to decide
Whose side to be on
The guys who wanted to start a race war
Or the guy who wanted to end it

DEAR FUTURE

I am Juan
I am barrio
I am Washington
I am ghetto
I don't ball
I don't bang
I am the neighborhood freak
And I have the beatdowns to prove it
I see a future
In my mind
In my heart
In my spirit
My heroes are Zapata
Malcolm X
And Che
I read
I write
About things that may not matter
But just might
I am legal
I am off into the world
Where I will be free
To be.

AFTER LINE 9

After line 9
Comes the inevitable
Inspiration
The second thought
The what if of it all
The moment of being
Surprised
Amazed
At the subconscious
Unfettered
Out of control
Firing on all four cylinders
Of just how brilliant it all feels
It's the moment of creative
Before it all comes crashing
Back to earth
While waiting for what happens
After line 10

TIME LOST

I came to
As a woman was wiping blood
From a gash in my head
Time lost
30 minutes
I came to
As a woman was making the sign of the
cross
And giving me last rites
Time lost
15 minutes
I came to with an oxygen mask over my
face
And somebody saying
Do you know where you are?
Time lost
10 minutes
I came to
With a gun in my hand
Five shots fired
One in the chamber
Time lost
Eternity.

THE NIGHT BEFORE CHRISTMAS

It was the night before Christmas
I had the milk
But was out of the sugary sweet
Cookies
So I left some dark, erotic poetry instead
The next morning the milk was gone
As was the poetry
I hope Santa and the Mrs enjoyed them
During those cold winter nights

WRITING AS BLOOD SPORT

I once had an editor pull a gun on me
My crime?
Trying to collect $20
Back when $20 was the difference between
Top Ramen and a Happy Meal
A publisher once claimed I had threatened
to kill his secretary
Because he owed me a shitload more than
$20
Not true
He owed me the money
Not his secretary
And he was too far away
For me to get a clean shot
Three different magazines I was writing for
Went out of business on the same day
They didn't owe me much
But this was back in the day when
Very little was a lot
I recently sold a short story
And was paid on acceptance
Acceptance?
I know. It sounded like science fiction to
me too
The story was published

And the publication folded two days later
At that point I did what any hardworking
writer would do
I kept the money
And resold the story

WHO I AM

Who
Who
Who
I am
This is who I am
I am stoned
Immaculate
I shoot Starbucks and bad television into
my veins
I haven't slept in 19 months
This is who I am
I am war
I am peace
I save lives
I take lives
I was found hanging from a tree
I am a sinner
A saint
A victim
This is who I am
I live by the rules
I break the rules
I believe in god
But only my god
I embrace the day

I hide in the shadows
I am indivisible
I am invisible
This is who I am
The next day
The next
And the next after that
This is who I am
Yesterday
Today
Tomorrow
And forever

I SHOULD

I should do this
I should do that
This gets me what I want
That gets me what I need
This is my Jekyll
That is my Hyde
The sun is going down
There is not much time
What to do?
What to do?

AND THEY'RE OFF

It was the sixth race
The horses were rounding the clubhouse
turn
The 15-1 longshot looked promising
It had the pedigree
It had the jockey
Whose name I could not pronounce
So I laid my money down
A long anguished cry
Pierced the overcast
It was pleading from the cheap seats
For the favorite
Who was beginning to fade
As my longshot began to make its move
On the favorite's left
There was pain
And fear
This wasn't just another two dollar slouch
Playing at drama queen
This was somebody who had just bet the
rent money
Who had just bet the farm
Who needed a fix
Who might soon be getting a knock on the
door

From unpleasant bone breakers
On call from an equally unpleasant shylock
The horses were neck and neck
With a couple of hundred yards to go
His screams were beyond frantic
Bordering on apoplectic
My longshot went ahead by a nose
I turned in the direction of the deep seats
Just as the screamer went over the rail
Splattering on the level below
As the sign on the jumbotron flashed
Photo finish

CAN'T TRUST THAT DAY

Do not go easy into Sunday
It is not a pretty sight
The brain is hotwired to 24/7
Your loved ones say enough already
Even God took a day off
But what happens when you are not God?
This...
You attempt the mundane
The mindless
You mow the lawn
Grass clippings do not deaden the urge
But rather sharpen it to razor clarity
A good book
Generates the mental shakes
Because you know you can do better
Walk
Pace
Annoy your wife
And when all else fails
Check your email
If it's good news you're anxious to top it
If it's bad news you want to rush to
redemption
Finally you sleep
Or try to

You're thinking
Only hours left to Monday
When the hounds can be released
Once again

NIGHT RIDER

He got on the metro at the station
Barely avoiding being cut in half by the
closing door
He staggered down the aisle
A tipped up skateboard in one hand
A brown bottle of something called Kill
Liver in the other
He seemed crusty and dry
Unpredictable
Dangerous
Possibly armed
Physically and mentally
He looked like trouble
The passengers took the hint
Moving way to the other side of the train
He sat down
Hunched over
Mumbling and drooling
Dirty white boy afro seemingly frozen on
his head
A look that said nothing
Finally
I'm into hip hop
I'm into rhymes
To no one in particular

And no one who cared
I'm going to be famous one day
Still no response
He shrugged his shoulders
Retreated into his own madness
His clogged and clotted mind
Mentally scabbed over
And remembered the time
When he told people on a train
He was into the blues
And that one day he would be Willie Dixon
When he told people on a train
He was into rock
And that one day he would be Elvis
And that one day he would be The Beatles
Led Zeppelin
The Sex Pistols
Prince
His madness and his memories were
jogged as
The train hit the last stop on the line
Everybody exited
Ignoring his attempts to fist bump them as
they passed
Leaving him alone with his thoughts
Suddenly the train lurched forward
And into the night
As the rider contemplated his past

His present
And the eons spent going nowhere fast
On the train rocketing into his future
He lived in a world where madness always
had another chance
Stops went on forever
And hopes and dreams
Were his ticket to ride

NOW'S THE TIME TO SAY GOODBYE

When it's time to go
Most go quietly
Without a whimper
A tear
And a whole lot of regret
About the way things should have gone
For some the end plays out differently
One last smile
Leaving a footprint
A fossil
Memories that burn bright in the sky
A sign that in the end
It all meant something
In the fabric of time

IN 5 LINES

Some days you eat the bear
Some days the bear eats you
Some days nobody eats
It's life
Get used to it

THE C WORD

Contemplate
Concentrate
Concept
Conceit
Courage
Create
Conception
Contact
Contribute
Congratulate
Circle
Continues

POINT OF ORIGIN

Walking down the street
It used to be easy
It was hi
How ya' doin'?
How's the wife and kids?
Where did you say you're from?
No pain no strain
But then things got all street
All 2018
All territorial
And all dangerous
Where are you from?
Asking and answering
Can be a minefield
Where you're from can get you shot
Or deported
Or worse
So what is one to do
When telling somebody where you're from
Might get you on the wrong end of a drive
by
Shived
Or a visit from ICE?
Try this
Next time somebody asks

Where you're from
Just tell them
I'm from my mom and dad
That should get you off the hook
Because who's going to make an issue
Out of sex and life?

DARE TO SLEEP

Tried real hard
But could not make it
To the other side
3 a.m.
I am awake
Mind racing nowhere and everywhere
While the usual suspects
All night radio jibber jabber
Playing out in the blackness
Where nobody is listening
Except me
Memories of the good old days
Which upon further examination
Were not all that good
Just are not cutting it
Neither is tossing and turning
Or self -gratification
It's getting light
The paper should be thudding on the
driveway
The dog should be whining to go out
Worst case scenario
I'll probably doze off around 10 a.m.
Best case scenario
I'll have something to write about

TWO SPURS OF THE MOMENT

Just finished mowing the lawn
All hot and sweaty
Some people do this for a living
Now I know why I write

Getting ready to root for Croatia in the
world cup finals
Then my neighbor tells me he has a lot of
money
Riding on France
He gives me a bag of avocados from his
tree
I'm easy
Viva la France

GO GENTLE

She passed two years ago
It had been time enough to learn
To be alone
To cry and then not to cry
To talk to her ghost
And her memory
And to cringe at the idea
Of doing it all over again
He had tried many times
To take another's touch
That was not her touch
And going to his bed alone
Until the day he took a hand
That felt warm
Natural
Giving
No sense of guilt
Or Betrayal
He would not be alone this night
It was time to move on

MENTAL ETCH A SKETCH

I don't have tattoos
But my mind is inked
It screams hardcore shit
That I'll regret later
Jesus on a cross
Cuddling with serpents and hoochie mamas
Hearts and skulls
The names of long ago loves
Ragged gang slogans
And slave chains
The ying and the yang
The dreams and the nightmares
Things that scare me
Make me laugh
And make me wonder why
If I had immortalized them
With the needle
The ink
And the blood
They would be with me forever
But this way I can always flip
The mental Etch A Sketch
And start all over again

JUST A THOUGHT

Sun
Its rays
Drip like wild Pollock and Dali
On the canvas that is earth
And is us
What it means
Is in the eye of the beholder
And anybody's guess

GOD COMPLEX

I am patient zero
I'm the one to praise
I'm the one to blame
Because way back
I was the one
Who started it all

BIOGRAPHY

Existential Jibber Jabber is Marc Shapiro's first collection of poetry and his second publishing venture with DEMAIN PUBLISHING (his Short Sharp Shocks! book entitled *Let Me Take You Down* being the first). He is the author of more than ninety unauthorized celebrity biographies including, most recently, *Keanu Reeves' Excellent Adventure* (Riverdale Avenue Books) and *Word Up: The Life Of Amanda Gorman* (Riverdale Avenue Books). His vampire themed poetry and short stories have made regular appearances in the magazine *Night To Dawn*. He is a New York Times, Los Angeles Times and Canadian bestselling author. He is a published short story writer, poet and comic book writer. Marc Shapiro is a prolific so and so who is living proof that it is possible to make a living doing this. Don't tell the authorities. Now if you'll excuse me, it's time to mow the lawn and walk the dog.

ADRIAN BALDWIN (COVER ARTIST)

Adrian is a Mancunian now living and working in Wales. Back in the 1990s, he wrote for various TV shows/personalities: Smith & Jones, Clive Anderson, Brian Conley, Paul McKenna, Hale & Pace, Rory Bremner (and a few others). Wooo, get him! Since then, he has written three screenplays—one of which received generous financial backing from the Film Agency for Wales. Then along came the global recession which kicked the UK Film industry in the nuts. What a bummer! Not to be outdone, he turned to novel writing—which had always been his real dream—and, in particular, a genre he feels is often overlooked; a genre he has always been a fan of: Dark Comedy (sometimes referred to as Horror's weird cousin). *Barnacle Brat* (a dark comedy for grown-ups), his first novel won Indie Novel of the Year 2016 award; his second novel *Stanley Mccloud Must Die!* (more dark comedy for grown-ups) published in 2016 and his third: *The Snowman And The Scarecrow* (another dark comedy for grown-ups) published in 2018. Adrian Baldwin has also written and published a number of dark comedy short stories. He designs book covers too—not just for his own books but for a growing number of publishers. For more information on the award-winning author, check out:

https://adrianbaldwin.info/

DEMAIN PUBLISHING

To keep up to-date on all news DEMAIN (including future submission calls and releases) you can follow us in a number of ways:

BLOG:
www.demainpublishingblog.weebly.com

TWITTER:
@DemainPubUk

FACEBOOK PAGE:
Demain Publishing

INSTAGRAM:
demainpublishing